CAVITIES AND TOOTHACHES

ELAINE LANDAU

Marshall Cavendish
Benchmark
New York

Marshall Cavendish Benchmark
99 White Plains Road
Tarrytown, New York 10591
www.marshallcavendish.us

Expert Reader: Dr. Joel Berg, Professor, Lloyd and Kay Chapman Chair for Oral Health, Department of
Pediatric Dentistry, University of Washington School of Dentistry, Seattle, Washington

All Internet addresses were correct and accurate at the time of printing.

Library of Congress Cataloging-in-Publication Data
Landau, Elaine.
   Cavities and toothaches / by Elaine Landau.
        p. cm. — (Head-to-toe health)
   Summary: "Provides basic information about teeth, tooth decay, and the
benefits of good oral hygiene"—Provided by publisher.
   Includes bibliographical references and index.
   ISBN 978-0-7614-2848-0
   1. Teeth—Care and hygiene—Juvenile literature.   2. Dental
care—Juvenile literature.   3. Toothache—Juvenile literature.   I. Title.
RK63.L36 2008
617.6—dc22
2007019192

Editor: Christine Florie
Publisher: Michelle Bisson
Art Director: Anahid Hamparian
Series Designer: Alex Ferrari

Photo research by Connie Gardner

Cover photo by *Digital Vision/Getty Images*

The photographs in this book are used with the permission and through the courtesy of:
Super Stock: age fotostock, 4, 21, 22; *Photo Researchers:* Guillaume, 6; Carlyn Iverson, 9; Library of
Congress, 10; *Image Works:* Fotoware, 13; Bob Daemmrich 14; *Getty Images:* 3D4Medical.com; *Corbis:*
Peter Beck, 24; *Alamy:* Emillio Ereza, 25; *Phototake:* Dennis Kunkel, 17.

Printed in China
1 3 5 6 4 2

CONTENTS

TEETH ARE TERRIFIC

Imagine not having teeth. Your life would be very different. You couldn't eat an apple, or a hamburger, or popcorn. Pizza would be a thing of the past. You might not want baby food for lunch every day. Yet there would be little else you could eat.

You need your teeth. They help you tear and chew your food. But your teeth do more than that. They help you speak clearly and correctly. Healthy teeth and gums also help keep your whole body healthy. There's one more thing, too. Well-cared-for teeth can give you a great smile!

TINY, BUT TOOTHY!

Snails are extremely small. They have tiny mouths. Yet different types of snails can have hundreds to thousands of teeth. In fact, the average snail has 25,600 teeth! That's a lot of teeth to have in your mouth at one time.

The lower teeth usually come in before the upper teeth.

MAKE WAY—HERE COME YOUR TEETH

No one is born with a full set of teeth. Yet your teeth start to grow under your gums even before you are born. Your first teeth begin to show when you are about six months old. These are your **primary teeth**, or baby teeth.

By the time you are three years old, all of your baby teeth will be in. You will have twenty of them. At three years old, many more teeth could not fit in your mouth.

When you are about six years old, your baby teeth start to fall out. They are pushed out by your **permanent teeth**. By the time you are an adult, you will have thirty-two permanent teeth.

TOSSING TEETH

Children everywhere lose their baby teeth. People celebrate this in different ways. In Japan a baby tooth from the lower jaw is tossed over the roof. This is done so the new tooth will grow in upward and straight.

An upper tooth is tossed beneath the house. This is done so the new tooth will grow in downward and straight. This custom is followed in some other countries as well.

YOUR TEETH— INSIDE AND OUT

Question: What's the first thing you see when you open your mouth?

Answer: Two rows of teeth.

Bet that was your answer, too. But wait a minute. You aren't really seeing the whole picture.

The part of your tooth that you see is the **crown**. It has a hard outer covering of **enamel**. The enamel protects the tooth. But there is much more to your teeth than what you see.

Pretend you have X-ray vision. Then you could see under the enamel. There,

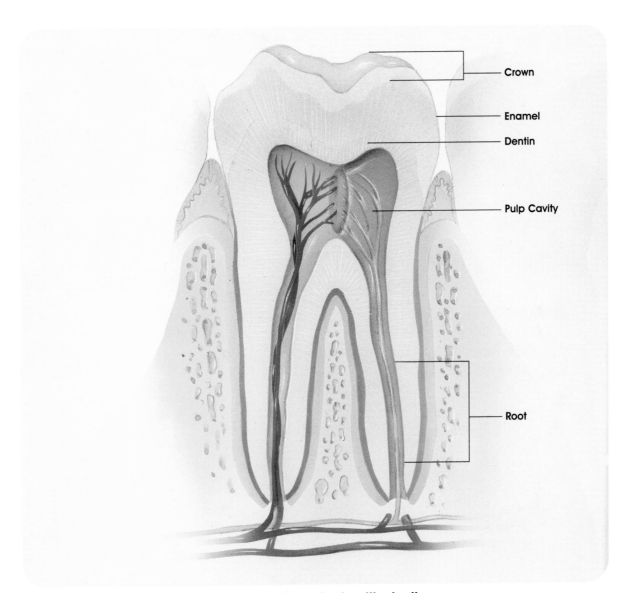

Crown

Enamel

Dentin

Pulp Cavity

Root

This illustration shows the layers and structure of a healthy tooth.

THE CASE OF THE MISSING TEETH

George Washington, our first president, lost all his teeth. So X-ray vision wouldn't help if you looked in his mouth. Washington had many sets of false teeth made for him. Some were carved out of elephant tusks. Other sets used cow teeth. Luckily, Washington never started mooing!

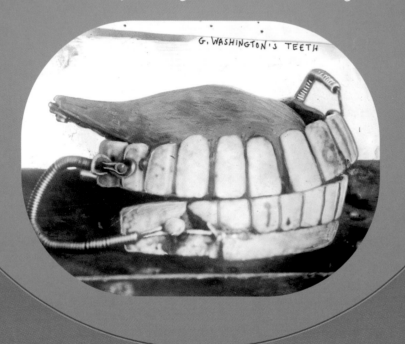

G. WASHINGTON'S TEETH

you'd find another hard substance, called **dentin**. Dentin is a little like bone. It protects the inside of the tooth.

Under the dentin is the soft center of the tooth known as the **pulp**. The pulp holds the tooth's nerve endings. Nerve endings are important. They let you know what's going on in your tooth. Let's say you fall off a swing and hit your teeth. The nerve endings would let you know that your teeth are hurt. Bam! You'd feel pain right away.

The pulp also holds the tooth's blood vessels. These feed the tooth and keep it alive in your mouth.

The tooth's roots hold the tooth in place. They reach down into the jawbone to do this. Each tooth can have one to three roots.

A layer of tough tissue called **cementum** covers most of the root. It serves as a sort of cement. It keeps the tooth's roots in the jawbone.

TYPES OF TEETH

In some ways your teeth are like a work crew. On a work crew, workers do different small jobs. Together, they get the big job done.

You may not think of your teeth as workers. Yet every time you chew something, they work for you. Like workers, teeth come in different shapes and sizes.

Together, your teeth make a great crew. They help you enjoy lots of different foods.

YOUR TEETH

Your front and center teeth are called incisors. You have four incisors on top. There are four on the bottom, too. Incisors are used to cut, tear, and chop food.

Can you spot the four sharp, pointed teeth next to your incisors? These are known as canines. Two are on top and two are on bottom. The top canines are sometimes also called eyeteeth. Canines help to tear your food, too.

Now open your mouth a little wider. See those fairly large, strong teeth with ridges on top? They are the ones next to

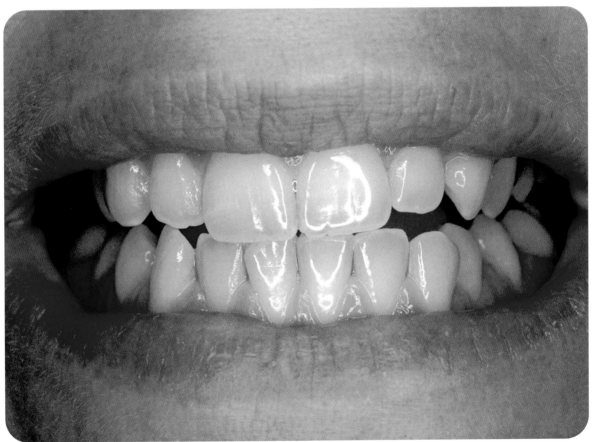

There are different types of teeth in your mouth. Each one has its own job.

DID YOU KNOW?

Right-handed people tend to chew their food on the right side of their mouth. Left-handed people tend to chew on the left side.

your canine teeth. These are premolars. You have a total of eight. Four are on the top and four are on the bottom. Premolars grind down your food.

Right next to your premolars are your molars. These look a lot like premolars, but they are even bigger and sturdier. You also have eight of these. Four are on the top and four are on the bottom. Molars smash and mash food. This is an important task. You can't swallow large chunks of food. You'd choke on them. But if you chew your food well, this won't happen. Your teeth see to that!

STAY AWAY DECAY

Millions of **bacteria**, or germs, live in your mouth. They are always there. They are just too small to see. When you eat, tiny bits of food are left in your mouth. These fall between your teeth or between your teeth and gums. The bacteria, along with the bits of food and other substances, form a whitish, sticky material on the surface of your teeth. It is called **plaque**.

Plaque is a real troublemaker. Whenever you eat anything sugary, the bacteria in the plaque spring into action. They gobble up the sugar and turn it into an acid.

SALIVA TO THE RESCUE!

There's a superhero in your mouth. It is the liquid called saliva. Saliva helps wash away any leftover bits of food. It also helps lessen the harmful acid created by bacteria.

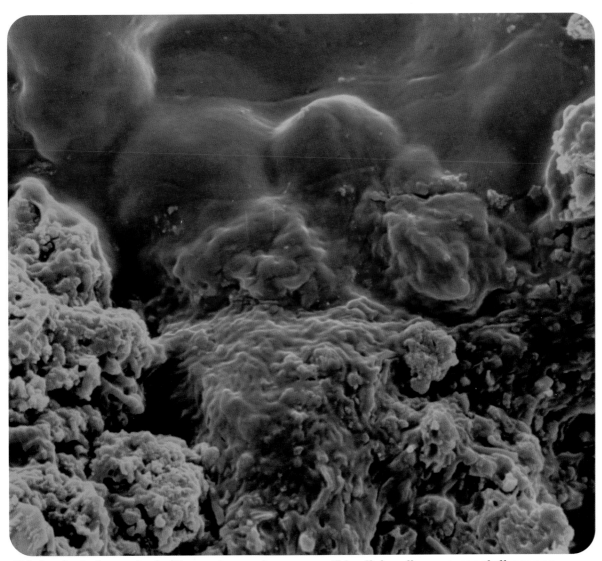

This is what plaque looks like under a microscope. This sticky, slimy, germy stuff causes cavities and gum disease.

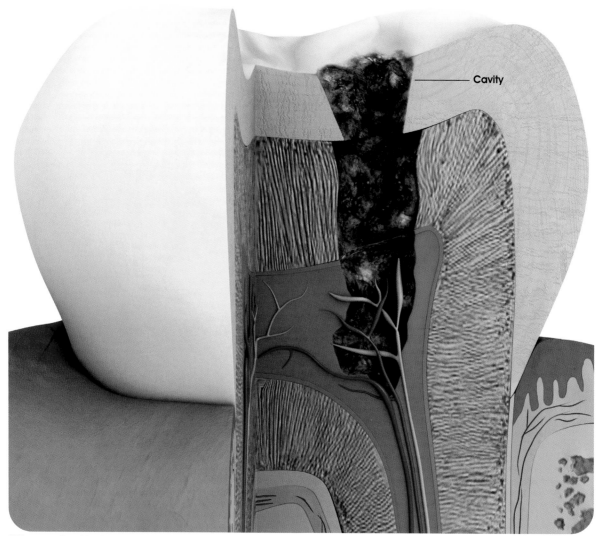

Cavity

When a tooth decays a cavity forms, creating a hole that grows deeper and deeper if it is not treated.

The acid causes tooth decay. It eats away at the enamel covering your teeth. When you finally have a large hole in the enamel, you have a **cavity**.

Cavities can turn into toothaches. After the acid eats away at your tooth's enamel, it attacks the dentin. Next, it goes on to the pulp. When the decay reaches a nerve, you'll know it! It can cause a very painful toothache.

One way to prevent cavities is to avoid gooey or chewy treats. These stick to your teeth longer than other foods. They fuel the bacteria that cause tooth decay.

Brushing your teeth after you eat helps prevent cavities, too. But what if you've eaten and can't brush? Try rinsing out your mouth with water, instead. This cannot take the place of brushing, but it's the next best thing.

Taking Care of Your Teeth

You can help keep your teeth healthy. Brush after each meal. Use toothpaste that has **fluoride** in it, too. If you can't brush that often, brush at least twice a day. Be sure to brush after you eat breakfast and before going to bed.

Brush your teeth the way they grow. That means brushing up and down—not sideways. Be sure you get to the hard-to-reach back teeth. Don't forget to brush the tops and sides of your teeth, too.

Brushing teeth correctly reduces the chances of tooth decay.

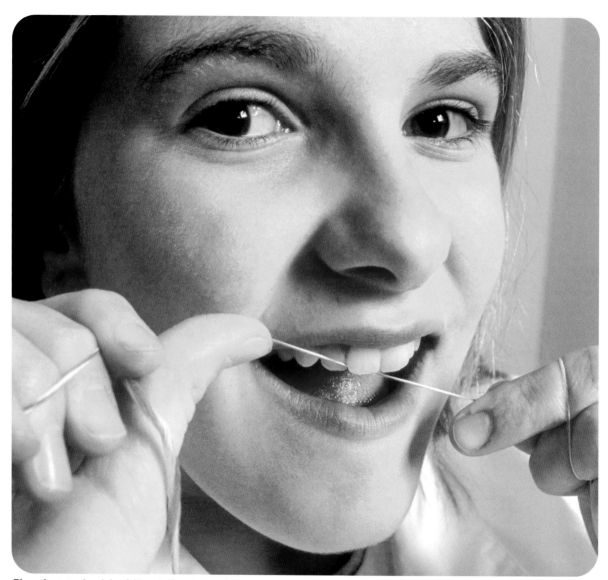

Flossing gets rid of tiny bits of food that your toothbrush cannot reach.

Brush gently, and don't rush. Most people brush their teeth for less than a minute. Yet it takes between two and three minutes to do a good job.

FLOSS? OF COURSE!

You need to floss, too. Gently work the floss between your teeth. Do this throughout your mouth. Flossing removes bits of food that your toothbrush can't get to. This lessens the buildup of plaque. Be sure to floss at least once a day.

Regular visits to the dentist are also important. You should see your dentist every six months. The dentist will look at your teeth and check for problems. X-rays or pictures of your teeth may be taken.

YOUR TOOTHBRUSH— DO'S AND DON'TS

After brushing your teeth, rinse off your brush well. This gets rid of any remaining toothpaste or dirt specks. Never share your toothbrush—not even with your best buddy or your brother or sister. You'll be sharing each other's germs as well. And don't even think of using your toothbrush on your dog or cat!

The X-rays will show if you have a cavity. If you do, your dentist will clean it out to get rid of the decay. Next, your dentist will fill the hole in your tooth left by the cavity. The filling material looks just like your tooth. When your filling dries, your tooth will be as good as new!

X-rays show the insides of your teeth and expose any hidden cavities.

SMART SNACK CHOICES

Healthy snacks are
good for your teeth. Some good
choices are

Fruits and nuts • Carrot sticks • Yogurt •
Cheese • Water or milk instead of soda

A **dental hygienist** at your dentist's office may also clean your teeth. The dental hygienist uses special tools to get rid of built-up plaque. Hardened plaque is known as **tartar**. Brushing alone will not completely remove it.

Some dentists keep a poster on the wall that reads "Ignore Your Teeth and They'll Go Away." That saying is funny, but it's true. It's a better idea to take good care of your teeth. You'll be glad you did. They'll last for the rest of your life.

GLOSSARY

bacteria — tiny germs that live in the mouth

cavity — a hole in a tooth caused by decay

cementum — a layer of tough tissue that covers most of a tooth's roots

crown — the outer part of the tooth that you see

dental hygienist — a person trained to clean teeth

dentin — a hard, bonelike substance that protects the inner tooth

enamel — the outer covering of a tooth that protects it

fluoride — a substance that helps fight tooth decay

permanent teeth — the second and final set of teeth to emerge

plaque — a whitish, sticky substance that collects on a tooth's surface

primary teeth — a person's first set of teeth

pulp — the soft center of a tooth that holds the tooth's nerve endings and blood vessels

tartar — hardened, built-up plaque

FIND OUT MORE

BOOKS

Chandra, Deborah, and Madeleine Comora. *George Washington's Teeth*. New York: Farrar, Straus and Giroux, 2003.

Civardi, Anne. *Going to the Dentist*. London: Usborne Books, 2005.

DeGezelle, Terri. *Taking Care of My Teeth*. Mankato, MN: Capstone Press, 2005.

Murkoff, Heidi. *What to Expect When You Go to the Dentist*. New York: HarperFestival, 2002.

Pirotta, Saviour. *Teeth*. North Mankato, MN: Smart Apple Media, 2003.

Royston, Angela. *Healthy Teeth*. Chicago: Heinemann Library, 2003.

Spilsbury, Louise. *Why Should I Brush My Teeth? and Other Questions About Healthy Teeth*. Chicago: Heinemann Library, 2003.

DVD

A Trip to the Dentist Through Pinatta's View. Big Kid Productions, 2004.

WEB SITES

Healthy Teeth

www.healthyteeth.org

A fun Web site with lots of information on keeping your teeth healthy.

Brushing Your Teeth

www.idph.state.il.us/HealthWellness/oralhlth/oralbrush.htm

A great guide to brushing your teeth correctly.

Dental Activity Pages For Kids

www.health.state.tn.us/kids/activity.htm

A super Web site with a brush and floss puzzle, and a healthy snacks maze.

INDEX

Page numbers in **boldface** are illustrations

About the Author

The award-winning author Elaine Landau has written over three hundred books for young readers. Many of these are on health and science topics.

Landau received a bachelor's degree in English and journalism from New York University and a master's degree in library and information science from Pratt Institute. You can visit Elaine Landau at her Web site: www.elainelandau.com.